Growing the Word of God Seed
How Spiritual Growth Works

ACKNOWLEDGEMENTS

First, I want to thank my mom for encouraging me to journal my thoughts at a young age, and as I got older, to step out of my comfort zone and share those thoughts with others.

Second, I want to thank those who listened to me teach and talk about this subject over the years. It is your kind words and feedback that led to this book.

Last, but never least, I want to thank my heavenly Father for showing me his truths though my adventures in learning to garden. He knows exactly what I need to keep plowing through the frustrations of my failed attempts at growing vegetables and celebrates my successes with me.

Copyright © 2018 Angela E. Powell

Scripture quotations are taken from the Holy Bible, New Living Translation, Copyright ©1996, 2004, 2015 by Tyndale House Foundation. Used by permission of Tyndale House Publishers, Inc., Carol Stream, Illinois 60188. All rights reserved.

Cover by Aaron Delarosa

All rights reserved. Except as permitted under U.S. Copyright Law, no part of this publication may be reproduced, distributed, or transmitted in any form or by any means, or stored in a database or retrieval system, without the prior written permission of the publisher.

ISBN: 978-0-9991594-2-2

Table Of Contents

INTRODUCTION	1
LESSON 1: THE PARABLE OF THE FARMER SCATTERING SEED	3
LESSON 2: THE FOOTPATH	8
LESSON 3: THE ROCKY SOIL	14
LESSON 4: THE WEEDY SOIL	21
LESSON 5: THE GOOD SOIL	27
LESSON 6: CHANGING THE SOIL	33
LESSON 7: TIME FOR TILLING	39
LEADER'S GUIDE	46
CONNECT WITH ME!	48

Introduction

I didn't enjoy gardening until I bought my first house. As a lover of classic Victorian era novels, I named the house Rosy Blessings because it had a lot of rose bushes. Learning to care for roses was my first gardening experience and many times, as I trimmed away dead stuff, the thorns left me with scratches and puncture wounds.

I soon discovered hidden treasures elsewhere in the yard as every spring new plants would surprise me. Some of these included the beautiful, yet somewhat alien looking Crown Imperial flower. Another was the Dragon Lily, which I found because of its horrible odor. These discoveries cultivated my curiosity for how plants grow and what they need to thrive.

This Bible study bloomed because of this magical garden. In my daily Bible reading I came across the parable of the sower. As I prayed about and studied this portion of scripture, the lessons I'd learned in my yard came to life in a new and profound way.

The parable of the sower is often used to show us where we've missed it in our spiritual walk, where we've hardened our hearts, and let the world distract us from our relationship with God.

But I believe there is so much more to this parable. I believe we can learn and understand how spiritual growth is supposed to work in our lives.

I know I've personally gotten frustrated when I've tried to change a certain behavior or habit I know doesn't please the Lord, and beat myself up whenever I mess up, or fall back into those old habits.

But this parable opened my eyes to see our spiritual walk as a journey. A journey of learning to partner with Jesus and other believers in our spiritual walk. In a lot of ways, this parable is about relationships. The relationship between the farmer and the seed, the seed and the ground it's sown into, and the ground and the farmer.

If you've ever felt stuck in your walk with the Lord, this study may help you get unstuck. It's not a self-help book, and it won't solve all of life's problems, but it can help you get out of the mud and understand that we can move forward in our relationship with Jesus.

Whether you're doing this study on your own, or with a group, I would encourage you to journal in a separate notebook. There are places for you to write thoughts down in this study, but in each lesson you are invited to spend time hearing what the Lord has to say to you and he may have more to say than fits on these pages. It can be beneficial to write down what he says so you can refer back to those words in the future.

Consider these pages to be your garden gloves and spade as we dig into the truths buried in scripture. Now, let's begin.

Lesson 1
The Parable of the Farmer Scattering Seed

"This is the meaning of the parable: The seed is God's word." (Luke 8:11 NLT)

As we go through this study, picture a garden in your mind. This could be a beautiful flower garden filled with all your favorite flowers, or a vegetable garden that provides delicious fruits and vegetables through the cold winter months. It could be a real garden you've seen before, or even the one you have in your backyard right now. Whatever type of garden you choose, I want you to do two things.

1. Invite Jesus into this place. Close your eyes and ask him to show you where he is in your garden. Take a few minutes and enjoy his presence there.

2. Get to know your garden. Explore it with Jesus. We will dig into the four different soil types in this parable. Every garden, big or small, has all four soil types in it. As we go through this study, I want you to picture finding each one somewhere in the garden you've created in your mind.

The parable of the farmer sowing seed is a well-known story and is documented in three of the four gospels. Often, it is used to show us areas that trip us up in our walk with God. That is not the goal of this study. Instead, we will take this passage of scripture and see how to use it to unlock our spiritual growth. We don't have to stay stuck in the rocky soil, or continue drowning in weeds. Through this parable, we can learn how to cultivate our spiritual walk and become the good soil, producing a harvest a hundred times more than was sown.

STUDY

Before we dig too deep, lets re-introduce ourselves to this story. Open your Bible and read the parable from Mark 4:3-20.

1. Can you identify what the three elements of this parable represent?

    The Farmer: _____
    The Seed: _____
    The Soil: _____

The question above is not meant to be a trick, but it can be difficult to identify what the elements represent even if you read all three accounts. I started this lesson by quoting Luke 8:11, which tells us the seed represents God's word. In, Mark 4:14 (NLT) we read, *"The farmer plants seed by taking God's word to others"*. This leaves us needing to identify the third element, the soil. This is found by looking at Jesus' explanation of each soil type.

2. Reread Luke 8:12-15. What phrase does Jesus repeat for each soil type?

_____

THE ELEMENTS

Let's break these elements down and make them relevant to us. The farmer is anyone who takes the word of God to others. Who do we take the word to right now? Who brings the word to us? The list for either question could be long or short. It could include our friends, parents, coworkers, extended family, and pastors. What about yourself? Were you in either of those lists?

We all have people in our lives we can share the word of God with, but many of us aren't comfortable doing so. This might be a lack of confidence, or a fear of being rejected. It could also be uncertainty in how to bring up our faith with people. Another reason could be we read this parable and identify with the rocky soil or the weedy soil and feel stuck in our spiritual growth, unsure we have anything of value to share with others.

3. Are you taking the word of God to others, or do you have a specific person or people you would eventually like to take the word of God to? Write their names below so you can ask God to show you how to more effectively take the word of God to them.

_____

_____

_____

_____

The seed is the word of God. That is pretty straight forward. If the farmer is someone who scatters word of God seeds to people, the word of God is acting as the thing being planted into the lives of others. This leads us to the soil types. They represent how the word of God is received in our lives.

Now, I realize this might twist your brain a little, but we can be a farmer who sows seeds AND the soil the seed is sown into. In Mark 16:15 Jesus tells us to, *"Go into all the world and preach the good news to everyone."* He wants all believers to sow the word of God into the lives of other people, but we also need the word sown into our own lives. We cannot give the word of God if it hasn't been given to us first.

So, the soil represents how each person receives the word of God. We'll dig deeper into this when we go through each soil type. For now, it's important to understand we can be both the giver of the word, and the receiver.

4. Thinking about the different soil types, how do you receive the word of God in your own life?

_____
_____
_____
_____

RELATIONSHIPS

This parable is all about relationships. You could say it's a fourth element in this parable. The farmer has a relationship with the ground (people) he's sowing into, and the ground (people) has varying levels of relationship with the farmer AND the word of God seed being sown into them.

A relationship is cultivated, just like a garden. Time is spent talking together, helping one another, and working through problems. The more willing we are to invest in a relationship, the better it will be. The same is true in our relationship with God and the Bible. The more time we invest in getting to know God, studying his word, and allowing him to lead us, the more we'll grow.

If we sow word of God seeds into the lives of other people, we need to be in relationship with them. If we receive word of God seeds from other people, we have a relationship with them.

Even if you listen to a teacher or preacher online or on T.V., there's a reason you listen to their message. Somewhere along the line, someone you know recommended them, or you trust they'll tell you the truth about the Bible. You may not know them personally, but you've learned enough about them to let them speak into your life.

Jesus uses the example of a garden to show us it's necessary for us to tend the word of God seeds we receive in our lives. Just like a gardener knows a tomato plant needs a lot of sun, while cauliflower needs more shade during the day, and each needs a different amount of water and will attract different pests. The word of God grows in our life when it's tended to.

APPLICATION

We've only introduced ourselves to the garden in our parable, we haven't smelled the earthy scent of freshly watered plants, or dug our fingers into the damp soil. But we're getting a picture of what this study will be.

I want to encourage you. Gardening can be messy, it takes work, but we don't have to figure it out on our own. There is an expert gardener standing by, waiting to reveal all the lessons the garden has for us to learn. Invite Jesus to join you on this journey. Ask him to help you understand the scriptures.

This study is not about our failures, it's about our growth and how we can get better at growing. Spend a few minutes imagining your garden each day, inviting Jesus to be there with you. Ask him where he is and pay attention to his expression and body language.

If this is a struggle, listen to some worship music, tell him what you're thankful for, and take deep breaths to calm your mind and body before asking Jesus into your garden.

How Spiritual Growth Works

Lesson 2
The Footpath

"A farmer went out to plant his seed. As he scattered it across his field, some seed fell on a footpath where it was stepped on, and the birds ate it." (Luke 8:5 NLT)

Every single person alive on earth today has a footpath in their lives. A place we smooth over and trample down so we can get from one place to another with ease. When something grows along our footpath, we rip it out or spray it with poison. The footpath is a place we protect from growth.

1. Before getting started with today's lesson, close your eyes and spend a few minutes with Jesus in the garden you created. Search for the footpath. What is it made of? Write your answer below.

_____

STUDY

Open your Bible and read Luke 8:5, 11-12. Then turn over and read Matthew 13:19.

Luke is the only gospel that gives us a picture of the seeds being stepped on as well as being eaten by the birds. Let's examine the word **stepped**.

In the Greek, the word **stepped** means **to trample down, to reject with disdain, and to tread underfoot.**

Matthew 13:19 explains that seeds on the footpath represent those who hear the message, but don't understand it. Then the evil one comes and snatches away the seed.

Luke 8:12 tells us the devil steals the seed to prevent the person receiving the word from believing it and being saved.

SEED FREE ZONE

Each gospel has a slightly different explanation for the footpath, but one thing is the same. The footpath is a seed free zone.

2. What does Mark 4:15 say about the seed on the footpath?
_____

In lesson one, we learned each soil type represents how the word of God is received. Here, the word isn't received because it's stolen away by the devil, or rejected by the person it's given to.

THE STOLEN SEED

If Satan is stealing word of God seeds to prevent a person from believing and being saved, it's safe to say these people haven't accepted Jesus as their savior yet.

Note, that nowhere in this parable does it say anything grew on this footpath, which could cause us to be discouraged about sharing our faith with unbelievers. However, we've all seen dandelions poking through cracks on the sidewalk, so while the parable shows nothing growing along the footpath, it is possible.

Isn't that a beautiful, yet frustrating picture? Imagine sharing the word with an unbeliever for several years and seeing no fruit, but one day they ask you how to be saved. It's like throwing handfuls of seeds at a sidewalk for years and suddenly a small plant starts working its way through a crack. The flower that forms is the fruit from all those seeds. The fruit is their newfound understanding and belief in Jesus.

If we look at a footpath and tell ourselves there is no point trying to grow anything in that place because it will be stolen away, then for sure that person will never receive Jesus. But if we view the footpath as a part of our garden that only needs extra love and attention to incorporate into the rest of the garden, then we see potential, beauty, and worth.

3. Do you know any unbelievers in your life who appear to be a lost cause? Write their names, or something about them that reminds you of them if you aren't comfortable writing their name. Pray and ask God to form cracks in them where his word of God seeds can grow.

_____
_____
_____

THE STEPPED ON SEED

At the beginning of this lesson, we looked at the meaning of the word *stepped* from Luke 8:5. As a reminder, it means *to trample down, reject with disdain, and to tread underfoot.*

All of us have areas in our life we would rather not share with others, including God. We might have a painful memory we've stuffed into the far recesses of our mind, hoping we will never have to face it again. Or it could be the failures we see in ourselves that we try to hide. We put on a happy face so no one will see how we're really feeling.

We keep these feelings, memories, and events locked in a closet with padlocks on the door and say "God, I don't want you involved in this area of my life." Or "I'm not ready to deal with this yet."

Whenever someone tries to sow seeds into those areas, it can be easy for Satan to come in and take it away. But we can't blame everything on the devil. We can also step on, or reject, the word of God seeds sown into our lives.

There are multiple ways we can do this. We don't trust the person giving us the word, or we don't believe the same things they do, so we find it hard to receive from them.

It might have nothing to do with the person giving us the word though. It could be we're afraid God will reject us or be angry with us if we show him this dark place we keep locked inside ourselves.

4. Can you think of an area in your life you've kept "seed free"? Write it down, then picture your garden in your mind. Ask Jesus to show you where he is in your garden. Spend time in his presence and ask him to help you understand why you've kept that area protected from seeds. I would encourage you to write down anything he tells you.

Remember we can receive the word of God in each of the four soil types, so don't be discouraged if you see areas that are seed free.

_____
_____
_____
_____
_____
_____

RELATIONSHIP STATUS

In lesson one, we saw how this parable is all about relationships. When it comes to the footpath, relationships can look pretty shaky.

A believer and an unbeliever can be great friends, but when it comes to our faith, there may be some awkwardness. We may hold to the saying, "Never discuss politics or religion in polite company".

How Spiritual Growth Works

If your faith is a large part of your life, then having unbelieving friends who don't want to hear about what you believe can be difficult, but not impossible.

If we view ourselves as being the footpath, we might not feel comfortable being vulnerable with the Lord for fear of his wrath and judgment. Or we might not see the value of taking our painful memories to him, it appears easier to keep them hidden away.

These suggest a weak relationship with the Lord. In other words, we don't know him very well. God wants to heal the wounds from our past. He wants us to know he loves us and it's safe to bring everything to him. God wants to be in relationship with us, all the time. A deep, intimate, life giving relationship.

5. Read John 15:5-6. Think about how our relationship with the Lord is like a plant. The more developed the root system (God), the more life the plant has (us), but only if the plant is connected to the roots. A picked flower can only survive in a vase full of water for so long before it dies.

Think of an area in your life in which you feel connected to God. Write it below. Can you think of any areas of your life in which you don't feel connected to the Lord? Are any of them seed free zones?

_____
_____
_____
_____

APPLICATION

It doesn't matter how long you've been walking with the Lord, we all have places in our life where we can grow and mature. Some people may have more seed free zones than others, but we all have them. God wants you to invite him into those areas, but it may take time before we're ready. We may not even be able to identify them yet. God knows and understands this and he still loves you, regardless.

If you've identified a seed free zone in your life, you don't have to throw the doors open and face it all at once. Instead, ask God to help you understand why you're reluctant to let him in. Then ask him to help you reach a place where you want to let him in.

Later in this study we will discover more about how we can change the soil in every area of our lives so it can become good soil that produces a harvest.

Lesson 3
The Rocky Soil

"The seed on the rocky soil represents those who hear the message and immediately receive it with joy." (Mark 4:16 NLT)

Getting plants to take root in rocky soil takes a lot of effort and determination. It's not an impossible task, but if we remove the rock, the job becomes a thousand times easier. The same is true if you start with a seed. Depending on the size of the seed, digging a hole big enough and deep enough could be a challenge in rocky terrain.

1. Picture your garden in your mind. Find the rocky area. It will most likely have a few plants in it, but not many. Invite Jesus to see this part of your garden with you. Write a short description of what this area looks like.

_____
_____
_____
_____

STUDY

Open your Bible and read Mark 4:5-6, 16-17, then turn over and read Luke 8:13.

Have you ever read something in the Bible, or heard a message and been in awe of the profound, yet simple truth of what you learned? It's exciting.

It's even more exciting when you share what you learned with someone else and they understand it too.

But what happens when we share and the response is lackluster, or the person we're sharing with asks questions we don't know how to answer yet, or rejects the truth we've just learned? It can feel like someone threw a blanket over our fire.

THE BELIEVERS JOURNEY

In the last lesson, we looked at the journey of a new believer. First with the idea that a flower growing through a crack in a sidewalk represents an unbeliever being saved.

If we continue with this theme, we could view the rocky soil as representing a new believer who is excited about everything they're learning in the Bible and at church. But when they encounter people who aren't as excited as they are, or they're rejected for what they're learning, it can smother their joy and they stop talking to people about what they're learning.

Sometimes, they may stop learning altogether because their motivation has disappeared. It's no longer fun to learn about God and the Bible when they keep getting rejected because of it. So they wither away, just like the plant in the rocky soil.

2. Can you think of a time when you shared something you were excited about and no one else seemed to catch your excitement? Write about it here.

_____

_____

_____

How Spiritual Growth Works

JOY AND DISAPPOINTMENT

While it's true, many new believers go through a rocky soil phase, we all experience problems in life that seem bigger than God.

Luke 8:13 tells us the word of God seed withers because we face temptation and fall away.

3. What do Matthew and Mark say about the withered word of God seed? Matthew 13:21; Mark 4:17.

_____

_____

_____

Everyone has problems. Imagine the rocky area of your garden for a moment. Think of the rocks as the problems of life, now imagine you're holding a tiny seedling in your hand that has only been growing a few weeks. If your plan is to plant this precious, tender sprout in the rocky soil, are you going to look at the rocks and think, "this is impossible"? Or, are you going to remove rocks to make space for the plant?

Most of us would remove the rocks, but when we see the problems of life and compare them to our knowledge of the Bible, our problems seem bigger than what God can do for us. In other words, we make the rocks more important than the plant.

4. Read John 14:27. In this passage, Jesus is telling the disciples he will send the Holy Spirit to them after he leaves. He tells them not to be troubled or afraid.

Consider the times you've been troubled or afraid. Were you able to go to God and give him whatever it was you were troubled about or afraid of? Why can it be so hard to do this?

_____
_____
_____
_____
_____

TEMPTATION AND PERSECUTION

There are many temptations in life. It's tempting to binge watch T.V. shows in the evening, or sleep for another ten minutes in the morning instead of studying the word of God. It's tempting to ignore the whisper inside telling us to talk to our coworker about God. It's tempting to accept a job offer that will allow us to buy anything we've ever wanted, but will require us to work longer hours and spend more time away from our families.

Temptations come in all shapes, sizes, and forms. But again, if we see the rocks in our garden as temptations, which is more important? Giving into the temptation and making it more important than the word of God? Or is tending to the word of God seed that's been planted in our lives more important?

5. What are things that distract or tempt you away from reading the Bible or praying? List those things below and ask God to help you refocus your priorities and choose the plant over the rock.

_____
_____
_____

The definition of the word *persecution* is *hostility and ill-treatment, especially because of race, political or religious beliefs.* In the Greek, the word refers to *those seeking to punish God's messenger with a vengeance like a hunger trying to conquer or obliterate someone as their catch.*

Most of us don't get persecuted to that degree, but it's likely we've experienced or heard of someone getting into an argument about their beliefs, or lack thereof, in God. Hurtful words are exchanged because we feel the need to defend ourselves, but nine times out of ten, the argument leaves us disappointed.

6. Have you ever shared your faith with someone (online or in person) and been rejected, or have you ever been in an argument as described above? How does the disappointment affect how you approach the next opportunity to share your faith?

_____
_____
_____
_____
_____

RELATIONSHIP STATUS

When rocks (problems) seem bigger and more important than the plant (word of God), we may have immature plant growth in our lives. Imagine the difference if we were trying to plant a young tree in the rocky soil. We might get a tool to help us dig through the rock because the size of the hole we'd need would be much larger than the one we'd need for a tree seed.

The value we place on the effort involved can change when the plant size changes. We know planting a flowering bush will be worth it because we already see the fruit, but planting a seed or seedling, may not be worth it because we don't know what kind of fruit it will produce.

If we are just getting started on our journey with God, we may not understand the value of pursuing daily Bible reading and prayer because we don't know what kind of effect, if any, it will have on us down the road.

It could also be we've been walking with the Lord a long time and in some ways we've seen a lot of growth and in others, not much at all and we don't understand why. In this case, we've seen fruit in our lives in some areas, but in others problems seem to keep getting in the way and pile up so high it feels like we'll never be able to focus on the tiny plants growing there.

We may need to look at our relationship with the Lord. Do we lack knowledge about who he is and what he can do in these areas of our life? Have we had bad experiences in the past and we're afraid to trust him with those areas?

7. Can you think of some places in your life that seem a little rockier than others? Write them down, then pray and ask God to help you see what is causing those rocks to keep building up, and what you can do to refocus on the plants planted there.

_____

_____

_____

APPLICATION

Because we live in a fallen world, we all face problems. It's easy to get stuck in a rhythm of complaining about our problems instead of focusing on the good things God is doing in us.

How Spiritual Growth Works

   Write down things you appreciate. Coffee with a friend, not having to wait in line for gas, whatever it may be. Start a list and remind yourself often of things you appreciate.

   Find someone willing to do this with you. Whenever you catch each other complaining about problems, you can encourage each other to find something to appreciate in the situation.

Growing the Word of God Seed

Lesson 4
The Weedy Soil

"Other seed fell among thorns that grew up and choked out the tender plants so they produced no grain." (Mark 4:7 NLT)

No one likes to see weeds growing in their gardens. They create an ugly spot in the midst of orderly beauty. A good gardener knows the best time to pull weeds is when they're still small because the roots have not had a chance to get a good hold in the ground. Not to mention, many weeds can have thorns, prickly ends, or other unpleasant obstacles when they get to be a certain size.

1. Close your eyes and picture your garden. Invite Jesus to be there with you. Find a spot with weeds. How big are the weeds you've pictured in your garden? Ask Jesus to help you clear the ground around the good plants. Notice his body language as he does so. Write down what you notice.

_____
_____
_____
_____
_____

STUDY

Open your Bible and read Matthew 13:7, 22. Then turn over and read Luke 8:7, 14.

Imagine going out to your garden and finding a tall patch of grass has grown into a section of your garden. It doesn't add to the beauty, in fact it's a sore spot. So you begin pulling the grass out by the root. Now, imagine as you're pulling the grass out you see the leaves of a tulip plant. You're no longer simply weeding, you're on a mission to rescue this poor plant.

But when you finally clear the ground, you see the leaves of the tulip are twisted and yellow with brown spots on the edges. With time and care you hope the flower will develop and bloom, but it doesn't. This plant has been choked by the grass.

In the same way plants can be choked by overcrowding them, our spiritual walk can become choked. The word **choked** used in this parable means **to choke (of a seed overlaid by thorns and killed by them) to suffocate with water, to drown.**

In other words, we could say the plant is suffocated until it dies. All three gospels tell us the same thing about the weedy soil. *"The seed that fell among the thorns represents others who hear God's word, but all too quickly the message is crowded out by the worries of this life, the lure of wealth, and the desire for other things, so no fruit is produced."* (NLT)

2. Do you ever feel your spiritual walk has been suffocated, or do you ever feel stuck in your spiritual growth? Pray and ask God to show you three areas, or three times in your life when you've been stuck and have not seen growth. This does not have to be specifically spiritual. What got you unstuck? Ask God to help you with this if you can't think of anything.

_____
_____
_____
_____
_____

THE BELIEVERS JOURNEY

Through our study, we've looked at how a new believer might progress as they mature in their relationship with God. If we consider the weedy soil as the next step on this path, we might see a believer who has been saved for a while, reads their Bible regularly, and prays regularly. But the day-to-day worries of life, making sure our to-do's are done, making enough money to provide the luxuries of life we both need, and think we need, and all the things that keep us busy, choke out the message we hear on Sunday mornings.

This might be where a lot of us get stuck. In this day and age it's easy to worry. God knew this would be difficult for us and he provided many examples and declarations in the Bible that tell us not to worry, or fear.

3. Can you think of three verses that tell us not to worry? Write them down.

_____

_____

STUCK IN THE WEEDS

So why do we get stuck here? One way to help us figure this out is to take a few minutes to break down our day. There are 1440 minutes in a 24-hour period. If you get a solid 8 hours of sleep a night, you've used up 480 of those minutes leaving you with 960 minutes. Some research indicates we spend about an hour a day traveling, and another hour eating our meals.

If we include getting ready for the day that can be anywhere from 20 minutes to 90 minutes depending on if you have kids. On top of all these basic things, an 8 hour work day leaves us with 270 minutes, or 4.5 hours, in our day for spending time with our family, cleaning our house, helping kids with homework, watching our favorite T.V. shows, participating in sports or hobbies, going to the gym, and all the other things we have going on in our lives.

Of course, everyone's life is different, and these numbers change for each of us, but the fact remains we do a pretty good job filling up our time. We may read our Bibles and pray regularly, serve at church, or attend a Bible study or small group, but what happens after church is over? Do we remember what the sermon, or study was about a day or two later? Is it impacting our lives and helping us grow, or is church simply another category in our to-do list?

4. What fills your 1440 minutes in a day? If you have time, break your day down as best you can. You could also try it by breaking down your week into hours. There are 168 hours in a week. This exercise can help you identify when you have extra time to read the Bible, or identify wasted time.

_____
_____
_____
_____
_____
_____
_____
_____
_____
_____
_____
_____

RELATIONSHIP STATUS

At the beginning of this study, I stated it was not my goal to make anyone feel condemned or guilty. That is still the case. But in order to understand how we grow spiritually, we have to evaluate and recognize where we are so we can begin moving in the right direction.

When we're stuck in the weeds, we may feel we're doing all the right Christian things, but we're not seeing fruit. Bible reading and prayer are wonderful things, but are we allowing them to transform our lives?

Consider these verses from Philippians:

"Don't worry about anything; instead, pray about everything. Tell God what you need and thank him for all he has done. Then you will experience God's peace, which exceeds anything we can understand. His peace will guard your hearts and minds as you live in Christ Jesus." (Philippians 4:6-7 NLT)

We're told not to worry about anything, but to pray about everything. So when that bill comes due and you're not sure you can pay it, do you pray about it or try to figure out a solution on your own? What about when your child is doing something you don't approve of, or they're sick? What about rumors of lay-offs at work? Crime rates in your city? Again, there are so many things we can get caught worrying about.

When we get stuck in the weeds, sometimes we just need to look and see if we've gone to the Lord with those worries, and spend enough time with him so he can calm those worries, and remind us of who we are in him and who he is for us.

5. What is on your worry list right now? Write them down, then pray about them. Don't let it be a one sided conversation, let Jesus speak words of comfort to you and write them down. If it helps, imagine meeting with Jesus in your garden to discuss these worries. Pay attention to the expression on his face and his body language.

_____
_____
_____
_____
_____
_____
_____
_____
_____
_____

APPLICATION

In our last lesson, you started paying attention to things you appreciate. Continue practicing this. Whenever you find yourself worrying, look at the list of things you appreciate and spend a few minutes thanking God for those things.

The more you begin to appreciate the small things, the more you'll find the weeds of worry thinning. As we'll discover in our next lesson, the soil beneath those weeds can be very good.

Lesson 5

The Good Soil

"Still other seeds fell on fertile soil, and they produced a crop that was thirty, sixty, and even a hundred times as much as had been planted!" Matthew 13:8 NLT

For plants to thrive they need good soil. Good soil holds moisture, but allows excess water to drain and the soil provides nutrients to the plant through the plants root system.

Good soil requires work. Understanding what components make up good soil depends on the type of plants you're going to have in the soil. Some plants need more sand, others need more clay to thrive, and still others need an equal amount of all components.

1. Close your eyes and picture the garden you've created in your mind. Invite Jesus to be with you there, then find a spot where plants are thriving. Dig in the dirt with Jesus. Scoop up a handful of that good soil. Imagine what it might smell and feel like as it sifts through your fingers. What expression does Jesus have on his face as you do this with him? Describe all these sensations and emotions below.

_____
_____
_____
_____
_____
_____
_____
_____

STUDY

Open your Bible and read Luke 8:8, 15. Then turn over and read Matthew 13:8-9, 23

The good soil in this parable is everyone's favorite because it represents all things good. At the beginning of this study, we named the different elements in this parable and noted that the soil types are how we receive the word of God.

If we are receiving the word of God like good soil receives a seed, we hug that seed in a warm embrace, tending to it, and eagerly waiting to see those first leaves pop out of the ground. And when they finally do, we recognize the potential the plant has for future fruit in our lives so we check the area around it for weeds, check the plant for bugs and other pests that could destroy it, and if need be, we give the plant support so it doesn't fall over or break under the weight of the coming fruit.

2. Think about how this might apply to your spiritual walk. What do you loving care for in your walk with God? Do you guard your prayer or Bible reading time? Do you write down what God tells you? Or do you have Bible verses posted around your home to help you remember God's promises for us? List the things you do to tend your spiritual garden.

_____
_____
_____
_____

Knowing what it takes to turn average soil into good soil, allows us to apply the same principle to our own lives. It helps us better evaluate where we are in our relationship with Jesus and where we can improve.

Having good soil doesn't mean having perfect soil. It simply means we take care of the soil, or we're taking care of how we receive the word of God seeds planted in our lives. Rocks (problems) and weeds (worries) are always going to pop up, but we can choose how we look at those issues. Are we going to get overwhelmed whenever we see a rock or weed in our garden, or are we going to pluck it and toss it out because we know the plants growing there are more important and bring life to us?

CHANGING THE SOIL

By now you might be thinking this all sounds really great, but how do we change how we're receiving the word of God? The rest of this lesson, and the next two are going to focus on this.

One thing to make mention of, is soil can be amended at any time. Before seeds have been planted, when plants are just sprouting from the ground, and after plants have grown big and tall. This does not require you to start from scratch. You don't have to re-evaluate everything you've ever learned about God, or pull out all the word of God plants that have been established in your garden and start over.

The only thing we have to do is choose to begin. It will be work, but it doesn't all have to be done right now. Remember, we all have areas in our lives that are footpaths, rocky areas, weedy areas, *and* good soil areas. Start by identifying the good soil. These are things you can go back to when the other areas feel difficult. A place to rest and encourage yourself before getting back to work. You started this by answering question number 2 in this lesson.

Once you've identified good soil, find a small patch of weedy or rocky soil. This might be one or two things you're struggling with.

How Spiritual Growth Works

Maybe it's a problem you're facing at work, or a worry that occasionally pops up in your life. It's possible you've already identified some of these areas in previous lessons.

3. What is one problem or worry you want to work on right now?
_____
_____
_____

Here are some practical tips on how to begin changing the soil in this one area.

1. After you've identified one or two small things you can work on, commit to pulling out those rocks or weeds. What does that look like? Pray about it, constantly. Every time you notice your need to deal with the problem pray about it. Every time you notice yourself worrying about that one thing, pray about it. If you aren't sure how to pray and you have your prayer language, pray in tongues and ask God to help you ask him the right questions.

2. Spend time each day listening for God's voice about that specific issue. Tell him how you're feeling, why you're feeling that way and ask for his guidance. Ask him to help you face the problem, or not worry when that situation comes up again. If it helps you, journal about it so you can go back and remind yourself what the Lord has told you about that situation.

3. Be aware of how you're responding to the situations, write those things down so you'll remember and can take them to the Lord when you have time.

4. Remember, you're tending a word of God seed as you do these things. Imagine what that seed is going to grow into in the future. Ask God to show you what the fruit of that seed is going to look like.

4. Let's get practical here. Life is busy, and even if we start small, this process can seem hard. Think of two ways you can start being more aware of how you're responding to the problem or worry you want to work on and remind yourself to pray and get God's opinion on the matter. This could be something as simple as writing yourself a note and posting it in several places to remind you throughout the day. Or committing to pray and journal about it each morning or evening.

_____
_____
_____

    Changing soil is a process. It's a balance. Making yourself more aware of how you respond to a situation could bring discouragement. We need to balance that with encouragement.
    Finding appreciation in every situation is one way to do this. Another is by going to the garden you've created in your mind, inviting Jesus to be there with you, and simply resting in his presence. Worship music and prayer are also great ways of encouraging ourselves.

5. What are some ways you can encourage yourself when you begin to feel discouraged?

_____
_____
_____
_____

APPLICATION

In the next two lessons we'll go into much more detail about how we can change the way we receive the word of God. For now, be aware of that small patch of rocky or weedy soil you want to work on, keep finding things to appreciate, and perhaps begin to find ways to show appreciation to other people, and encourage yourself in the Lord.

By taking these first steps, you have approached that small section of your garden, have identified what kind of soil you're working with, and you've figured out ways to begin changing the soil. In the next lesson, we're going to discover how God has already provided us with help in turning this rocky or weedy soil patch into good soil.

Lesson 6
Changing the Soil

"It is the same with my word. I send it out, and it always produces fruit. It will accomplish all I want it to, and it will prosper everywhere I send it." Isaiah 55:11 NLT

Composting is the act of setting aside organic material so it can decay and be used to add missing nutrients to soil. When most people think about compost, they think of something that smells really bad.

There are right and wrong ways to create a compost pile, and the experts all say the right way of doing it doesn't cause an overwhelming odor. They also know the benefit of compost far outweighs any smell that might come from it.

STUDY

Open your Bible and read Isaiah 55:8-13.

1. Consider Isaiah 55:8. We tend to view the footpaths, rocky, and weedy areas of our lives as things we've failed at. Take a few moments and ask God what his thoughts are about those areas in your life. Write down what he says.

_____
_____
_____
_____
_____
_____

How Spiritual Growth Works

We've discussed, in detail, the four different types of soil mentioned in the parable of the sower. All of them, except the footpath have plants that grew, at least a little. But as we talked about in lesson two, we've all seen dandelions growing through cracks in a sidewalk, so we know it's possible for plants to grow there.

Jesus doesn't say this in the parable because he's trying to make the point of Satan interfering by stealing the word of God. Another thing we need to see in this parable, is in every situation where a plant grows, except in the good soil, a plant also dies.

On the footpath, if a plant were to grow there, it would be trampled and die. In the rocky soil, the plant springs up, then withers away. The weedy soil doesn't specifically say anything about a plant dying, but the plant doesn't produce fruit and is choked out by the weeds. Anything choked long enough will die.

We don't see death in the good soil because plants stay healthy and are able to produce fruit continually, but let's consider a couple of verses in Isaiah 55.

2. Read Isaiah 55:10-11. How can we reconcile what verse 11 says with the idea that the word of God seed in Jesus' parable dies?

_____
_____
_____
_____
_____

LIFE TO DEATH TO LIFE

Compost is made up of dead organic material. We add it to soil that has lost certain nutrients in order to replenish those nutrients.

Compost helps create good soil and it helps plants grow bigger, stronger, and produce more fruit.

So what does this mean for us? Take a minute and consider how long you've heard the word of God. If you're a new believer, maybe it hasn't been very long, but if you accepted Jesus at a young age, it's likely you've heard the word of God taught hundreds, maybe even thousands of times.

Every sermon at church, on T.V., or online is an opportunity for word of God seeds to be planted in your life. Every friend who's shared what they've been reading and learning about in the Bible, or sharing what God has been speaking to them are also opportunities for Word of God seeds to be planted.

Now imagine you've had one hundred word of God seeds planted in your life and ninety-five of them have sprouted and died. That means you have a layer of compost that has collected on top of the rocky or weedy soil. The only thing that needs to happen in order for the soil to be amended, is to mix in the compost.

3. Take a moment and think of a time in your spiritual walk where you "missed it", let fear talk you out of doing what God asked you to do, or a time when you struggled to believe something in the Bible. If each one of those was a word of God seed that died, how can that dead plant material help you in the future?

_____

_____

_____

It's important to note we cannot change the soil by ourselves. Consider how many times you've determined to read your Bible every day. You start out really well, then after a little while you miss a day, then two, then three.

Willpower is important and can be helpful, but willpower alone will not help us change how we receive the word of God into our lives.

The more seeds we have scatted in our lives that sprout and die, the more compost we have to help create better soil conditions. But if the compost isn't mixed into the soil, it won't do us much good.

In fact, if you dump a bunch of compost on top of a garden bed, then plant seeds directly into the compost without mixing it into the rest of the soil first, your seeds will be waterlogged because compost is not great at draining excess water.

This tells us when we get a certain amount of compost piled up, it needs to be mixed in. We don't always know the best timing for this, but God does. He knows exactly how many word of God seeds have been planted in each of our lives, he knows how big the plants grew before they died, and he knows the exact moment when that compost needs to be mixed into the soil beneath.

Taking all this into consideration, we can see how God can use the dead word of God plants and use them to create life for future seeds. As the compost accumulates, and is mixed in, the better the soil becomes, which means future word of God seeds will have a better chance of growing and producing fruit.

RELATIONSHIP STATUS

In lesson one, we talked about how this parable is all about relationships. The farmer has a relationship with the ground (people) he's sowing into, and the ground (people) has varying levels of relationship with the farmer AND the word of God seed being sown into them.

We will not change how we receive the word of God by trying to do it on our own, and God can't change how we receive his word without our cooperation. Changing the soil is a partnership between us and our heavenly Father.

Our job is to believe we can change with God's help. It will take time (patience), effort, and a willing heart, but the rest is up to God. As long as we are willing to let God work in our lives, he will.

God's job is to know when it's time for the soil to be tilled, and present us with opportunities for tilling. Lesson seven will go into what this looks like in more detail.

4. Are you willing to let God work in your life? Is there anything that causes you to hesitate? Sometimes we need to start by asking God to help us be willing. See if you can identify any of these areas that make you hesitate. Write them down and ask God to show you why you're hesitating.

_____
_____
_____
_____
_____
_____

APPLICATION

When we look at a patch of soil teeming with rocks, or weeds, it can be overwhelming to even think about the process of clearing it all out on our own.

But when an expert gardener comes along, dumps compost on the area and brings out a rototiller, our confidence comes back. Suddenly it's not so difficult because the expert gardener is there to do the hard work and the only thing he requires of us, is that we're willing to help him.

How Spiritual Growth Works

Consider those hard things you've faced and felt defeated about in your walk with the Lord. How much easier would that problem become if you had an expert take over, so all you had to do was help?

Ask our heavenly Father, the expert gardener, to take over a situation for you. Trust he knows what to do and anytime you feel anxious or fearful, and feel the need to take those reigns back into your own hands, remember, your job is simply to help. Ask God how you can help him in this situation. Not by taking it out of his hands and attempting to do it all yourself, but by partnering with him, letting him show you the right way to go.

You may need to spend some quiet time praying and listening for his voice, journaling what he tells you so you can remind yourself when those anxious and fearful thoughts pop up, or looking for things to thank him for and appreciate as he takes you through this journey. Remind yourself that God knows the best timing for everything and if you don't see the expected results when you expected them, his thoughts and ways are higher than ours.

Growing the Word of God Seed

Lesson 7
Time for Tilling

"Where once there were thorns, cypress trees will grow. Where nettles grew, myrtles will sprout up. These events will bring great honor to the Lord's name; they will be an everlasting sign of his power and love." Isaiah 55:13 (NLT)

Tilling soil too long, or too often can actually take nutrients out of the soil, causing it to clump and harden. An expert gardener knows how to read the soil conditions to ensure the perfect amount of tilling.

STUDY

Open your Bible and read Acts 9:1-19

We're nearing the end of our study on how to grow word of God seeds. We've discussed the four soil types and how they represent the different ways we can receive God's word into our lives.

In the last lesson we went into detail about how those word of God plants can assist us in our spiritual walk even if they die, by turning into compost that can help future word of God seeds grow bigger and stronger.

Now, we're going to look at what it means to have our soil tilled. As we mentioned in the last lesson, the compost piled on top of the rocky and weedy areas of our lives needs to be mixed into the soil to amend it and make it better.

1. Take a few moments and picture the garden you've created in your mind. Invite Jesus to be there with you. Now picture a plot of land that needs to be tilled and keep in mind that what is truly

being tilled, is the way we receive God's word. What is your first reaction to how this might feel? What do you notice about Jesus' expression and body language as he prepares to till the soil?

_____
_____
_____
_____
_____

Tilling is a partnership. God knows the best timing for us to be tilled, and throughout our lives he presents us with opportunities to be tilled. We will look at several scriptural examples of people who were given this opportunity and see what that might look like in our own lives.

SAUL TO PAUL

Paul's conversion in Acts 9 is pretty intense. A bright light, a voice from heaven, blindness, and then a man who comes to restore his sight tells him it was Jesus who spoke to him on the road and he wants Saul to be filled with the Holy Spirit.

It's obvious by Saul's actions he's shocked and disturbed by these events. For three days he doesn't eat or drink (vs 9) and he spends the whole time praying. (vs 11).

Imagine for a moment what might be going through this man's mind. He's well educated in the law and he truly believes he's honoring God by killing Christians. Now he's blind, and probably wondering what sin he committed to bring this on, and God sends Ananias, a Christian, to help Saul begin to understand.

God provided Saul with an opportunity to be tilled. The law was always meant to point the Jews to Jesus, but they got so wrapped up in the do's and don'ts, they missed him. Their works acted like dead plant matter, and Saul had a lot of it.

He could have heard what Ananias and the other believers said, rejected it, rounded them all up, and taken them to Jerusalem to be killed. But whatever the believers told him while he stayed there, along with his Jesus encounter, convinced him he needed to be tilled and he was willing to let it happen.

2. Read Galatians 1:18-24. How much time did Paul spend learning to understand the scriptures, and the calling God had on his life before reaching out to the churches?

_____

_____

God tilled Saul, the well educated Pharisee who received the word of God as something to be obeyed to the letter and if it wasn't, punishment was certain. Because of that process, he became Paul, who is believed to have written at least thirteen books of the New Testament and became a man who offered grace instead of judgment.

PETER THE ROCK

3. Read Acts 2:38-41. We don't specifically see a "tilling moment" with Peter, but this is the first time we see him speak boldly about Jesus since Jesus' death and resurrection. Considering what you know about Peter, what do you think his tilling might have been?

_____

_____

GIDEON: FROM FEARFUL TO WARRIOR

When God sends his angel to tell Gideon what he wants him to do, the angel finds him threshing wheat at the bottom of a winepress to hide from the Midianites. The angel greets him by saying, "Mighty hero, the Lord is with you!". (Judges 6:12)

Gideon responds by telling the angel his family is the weakest in his tribe, and he is the weakest in his family. God was giving him the opportunity to be tilled by telling Gideon he had the potential inside him to be mighty for the Lord. Gideon wasn't so sure about that, but he choose to (cautiously) move forward with what God told him and through that process, became exactly what God told him he would become. A mighty warrior for the Lord.

RELATIONSHIP STATUS

4. What kind of relationship did Saul, Peter, and Gideon have with God before their "tilling moment"?

_____
_____
_____

5. What kind of relationship did they have after their tilling moment?

_____
_____
_____

6. If you assigned each of these men a soil type before their tilling moment, which one would give them?

_____

_____

_____

It's likely these three men had several tilling moments throughout their lives that helped them change their relationship with the Lord from distant to close.

The same is true with us. Possibly, we could even say we all started our relationship with Jesus by being tilled. The moment we chose to accept him as our Savior is a time of tilling. A time of God breaking up the hardened footpath so we can better receive his word.

In order for anyone to be saved, word of God seeds must be planted in the life of the unbeliever. Many of those won't survive or find ground to take root in, but the ones that do, sprout up and die as, slowly, the unbeliever begins to understand who God really is. Then, when they're ready, God presents them with an opportunity to be tilled. An opportunity to accept him, or continue on in their unbelieving ways.

When an unbeliever accepts the Lord, they've been tilled because they now receive word of God seeds better.

Another tilling moment could be a time when God shows us we've been going through the motions of going to church, but haven't let any of the messages affect how we live. We are given the opportunity to grow and change and receive the word of God differently than we did before. This is a time of tilling.

7. Considering the examples we covered, is tilling always a painful thing? _____

THE PROCESS

So, how do we change the soil? How do we change how we receive the word of God in our lives?

The first step is we have to be willing. When we come across a problem (rock) we have to choose to focus on the word. Problems will never go away. Even in a thriving garden, rocks will pop up from time to time. We have to make the word of God more important than the problems.

We can make the word more important than problems by reading the Bible. But, not just reading it, studying it. However, don't make studying the Bible a chore. Instead, find someone to study with, start a Bible study with some church friends, and really dig into the word. Celebrate what each of you learn through the process and encourage each other when things get difficult.

Prayer is another important step in changing our soil. Not a one way conversation, but time spent talking to and hearing from our heavenly Father.

Relationships with other believers is also important, but it's not just making friends so we can have lunch dates or go to movies together. We need relationships in which we can talk about what we're learning in the Bible, share our weaknesses and be encouraged and prayed for by others. Remember, the parable of the farmer sowing seed, is all about relationships with God and with other believers who can sow word of God seeds into our lives.

APPLICATION

Changing how we receive the Word of God is not hard, but it does take effort and time. Just like it takes effort to take care of a garden and time for those plants to produce fruit.

Don't expect things to change overnight. Growing plants is a process, it happens over time. Enjoy getting to know our heavenly

Father, being in relationship with Him, and in relationship with each other.

We change our soil by staying in relationship with God and with other Christians. And we make sure the Word of God is at the center of both relationships.

If we make the choice to read the word, cultivate our relationship with God, share what God is showing us through the Bible, and encourage others to do the same, our soil will change and we will produce good fruit.

How Spiritual Growth Works

LEADER'S GUIDE

For those facilitating this Bible study in a group setting, here are some helpful suggestions to ensure success.

I would encourage you to first, read through each lesson in advance, and then go through it a second time and do the study.

Also, if you can, don't rush through as you're preparing. If you can arrive at the group with samples of your conversations with the Lord, it will help the others feel comfortable opening up and sharing, which will make the study more beneficial to everyone involved.

Encourage group members to think about their own gardening experiences as they relate to this study. If they've never gardened before, ask them to think about science projects they may have done in elementary school to learn how plants grow, or to think about someone they know who does garden.

Another option is to open the Bible study by having everyone plant a flower in a pot they can take home and care for during the remainder of the study.

Have everyone read the material in advance if possible. The group time should focus on discussing the lesson, the passage of scripture studied, and give enough time for everyone to share their experiences with the Lord.

Pray with and for your group and encourage everyone in your group to pray for each other. Remind them this study is all about relationships and encourage them to have lunch or coffee with someone in the group they don't know very well.

Whenever someone is sharing, encourage the group in active listening and don't allow anyone to respond with advice, criticism, or judgment.

If you have a large group, feel free to break them up into small groups for prayer times, or when you want people to talk about what they've heard from the Lord. Many times people will feel more comfortable sharing if they only have to share with a few people, instead of a room full.

There may be people in the group who have never been taught how to hear God's voice. It may be helpful to explain that God can speak to us through images he puts in our mind, we may be able to sense how he's feeling, or we may have a thought or idea that comes into our minds that we wouldn't have thought ourselves.

Have fun! While this study is aimed at learning to grow spiritually and may bring up some hard things people in the group are facing, don't be afraid to enjoy the growth process. Laugh a little, cry a little, and grow in your relationships with each other, and with our heavenly Father.

CONNECT WITH ME!

Follow me on Twitter: @AuthorAEPowell
Follow me on Facebook: facebook.com/AuthorA.E.Powell
Follow me on Instagram: @authoraepowell
Sign up for my newsletter: www.angelaepowell.com

LEAVE A REVIEW!

If you enjoyed this study and think others would enjoy it too, please leave a review.

Honest reviews help bring my books to the attention of other readers. I would be very appreciative if you could take a few minutes and leave a review on the books amazon page.

Thank you.

How Spiritual Growth Works

www.ingramcontent.com/pod-product-compliance
Lightning Source LLC
Chambersburg PA
CBHW050448010526
44118CB00013B/1736